29

29

0 5

17

This b

The loan

a further p

EcoWorks

HOW ELECTRIC AND HYBRID CARS WORK

Nick Hunter

W
FRANKLIN WATTS
LONDON • SYDNEY

Franklin Watts
First published in Great Britain in 2015 by The Watts Publishing Group

Produced by Calcium

Acknowledgements:
The publisher would like to thank the following for permission to reproduce photographs:
Cover: Dreamstime: Gyuszko. Inside: Audi: 24; Dreamstime: Lcro774, Madajimmy 5; Shutterstock:
8, Artens 2, 11, Stefan Ataman 19, Hung Chung Chih 21, Ron Ellis 10, Patrick Foto 28, James A.
Harris 22, Intrepix 16, Johnbraid 6, Zoran Karapancev 26, Kavram 17, Yuriy Kulik 9, LovelaceMedia
18, Susan Montgomery 12, Mypokcik 15, Nikonaft 7b, Federico Rostagno 23, Fedor Selivanov 14,
SF photo 27, Michel Stevelmans 25, SVLuma 7t, Maksim Toome 29, Topora 20, Faiz Zaki 1, 13.

Dewey number 629.2'293
ISBN 978 1 4451 3911 1

Printed in China

Franklin Watts
An imprint of
Hachette Children's Group
Part of The Watts Publishing Group
Carmelite House
50 Victoria Embankment
London EC4Y 0DZ

An Hachette UK Company
www.hachette.co.uk

www.franklinwatts.co.uk

Contents

Cars clean up

Have you heard of an electric or hybrid car? These cars are in the news all the time – you might have read about celebrities driving hybrid cars or seen pictures of them in magazines. So, what is so special about these cars and how do they work?

Take a look inside

Conventional cars have an internal combustion engine, which runs on petrol or diesel. An electric car is different – under the bonnet is an electric motor, which runs on electricity. The car is powered by batteries, which are recharged by plugging the car into an electric socket, just like recharging a mobile phone. A hybrid car uses two energy sources to power it – the most common hybrid cars have a petrol-powered engine and an electric motor.

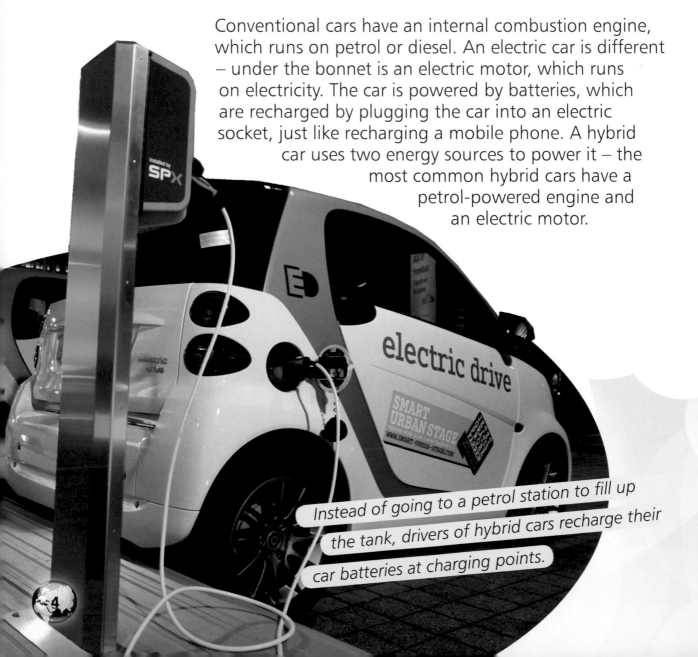

Instead of going to a petrol station to fill up the tank, drivers of hybrid cars recharge their car batteries at charging points.

Hybrids up close

The world's most popular and successful hybrid car is the Toyota Prius, which first appeared in Japan in 1997. Here are the important features that make the Prius such an environmentally friendly and highly economical car:

- Two power sources – a petrol engine and an electric motor.
- Each power source can operate on its own or in combination.
- The power changes automatically for the best performance.
- In town traffic, using the electric motor alone means zero emissions.
- When the petrol engine is running, it charges the battery.
- When the car brakes, the energy used goes back into the battery.
- The engine and motor switch off when the car stops, saving power.

The future is green

Hybrid and electric cars are just the start of a new wave of vehicles we are likely to see on our roads. These cars might be making the news today, but if the future really is environmentally friendly, they will be the commonly driven cars of tomorrow.

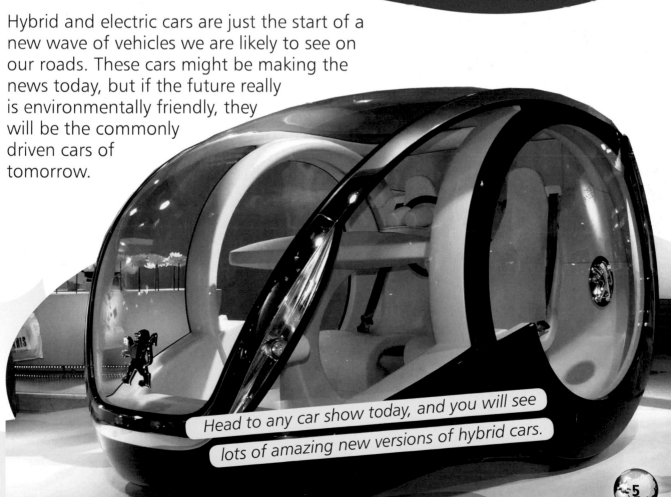

Head to any car show today, and you will see lots of amazing new versions of hybrid cars.

How cars work

Today there are nearly one billion cars on the road and most are powered by petrol or diesel engines. When they were first developed, internal combustion engines were noisy and unreliable. However, the engines were improved and soon they were used in almost all cars.

Burning fuel

Internal combustion engines get their name because fuel is burned (combusts) inside a sealed cylinder to drive the engine. An internal combustion engine is fuelled by petrol or diesel, which are extracted from crude oil and release lots of energy when burnt.

The Ford Model T, launched in 1908, was the most successful car of the early 1900s. It was powered by an internal combustion engine.

The perfect fuel?

Engines fuelled by petrol or
diesel allow cars to move at high
speed over long distances. The fuel can be
carried around in the car's fuel tank and the
cars are easy to refuel. However, petrol and
diesel also have some serious disadvantages.
The developers of hybrid cars are hoping that
they can provide a better alternative.

Some big modern cars with powerful engines can cover only a few kilometres for each litre of fuel they use.

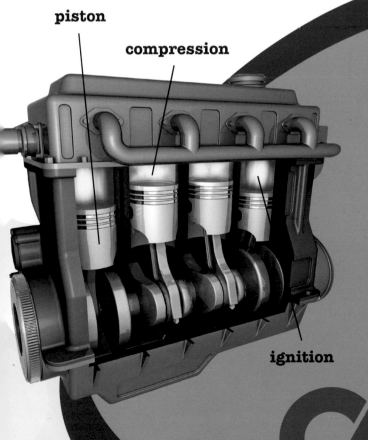

piston

compression

ignition

Internal combustion up close

In a petrol-fuelled internal combustion engine,
hundreds of tiny explosions take place every
minute to drive pistons and rotate the car's
wheels. This is usually a four-stage process:

- Intake: mix of petrol and air is taken
  into the cylinder.
- Compression: piston rises up through
  the cylinder to compress the fuel and
  create a more powerful explosion.
- Ignition: spark from a spark plug
  ignites the fuel, pushing the
  piston downwards.
- Exhaust: fumes created by the fuel
  are released from the cylinder, and
  the process begins again.

Car trouble

The invention of the internal combustion engine has changed the world. Cars give people the ability to travel further and it is hard to imagine our societies without them. However, conventional petrol-powered cars are the source of many problems in the modern world.

Lorries are powered by diesel engines. Like petrol, diesel comes from oil and causes air pollution.

The oil industry

The process of finding and refining petrol and diesel is one of the world's biggest industries. Petrol and diesel are extracted from crude oil. This oil is formed from the remains of living things that died millions of years ago. Once oil is all used up, it will be impossible to replace.

Searching for oil

Oil is found deep underground, and the process of drilling for oil often involves damaging some of the world's most delicate habitats. When things go wrong with oil exploration and transport, oil is spilled. Plants and animals can be killed and their habitats destroyed for ever.

Climate change

Oil pollution is not the only problem caused by conventional cars. They also have a huge impact on Earth's climate. Harmful fumes that pollute the atmosphere are released when petrol or diesel are burnt in a car engine. This changes the delicate balance of gases in Earth's atmosphere and, along with other polluters such as industry, is causing Earth to become warmer.

Warmer temperatures will cause more droughts. Millions of people will not be able to grow the crops they need to live.

The greenhouse effect up close

When fossil fuels, such as coal and oil, are burnt, they release carbon dioxide into the atmosphere. This gas is always present in the atmosphere. It is known as a greenhouse gas because it helps to prevent heat from the sun escaping into space, a little like a giant greenhouse. However, cars and industry are releasing too much carbon dioxide, so too much heat is being captured.

The electric option

Electric vehicles are now being developed by many different car companies, but they are still not a practical option for most car users. What is stopping full electric cars from appearing on our roads?

Already here

You may have seen electric vehicles without realising it. These are usually vehicles that are designed to travel small distances, such as delivery vehicles or forklift trucks. Small electric vehicles can also help elderly or disabled people to travel around their neighbourhoods.

Hybrid buses are used in many cities. They only need to travel at low speeds, and hybrid technology makes them quieter as well as reducing carbon emissions.

Early electrics

Many of the earliest cars were in fact electric. They were quiet and more reliable than early petrol engines. However, as cars became more popular, internal combustion engines became the only real option for most drivers. Electric cars could travel only short distances before they had to be plugged into an electrical source to recharge their batteries.

In the future, charging points may be as common as petrol stations.

ECO FACT

Electric drawbacks

Fully electric vehicles are limited because they need to be charged regularly. Of course, refuelling conventional cars is made possible only by a network of petrol stations. At present, there are a limited number of places where you can charge electric cars, and charging takes much longer than filling a tank with petrol or diesel.

Types of hybrid car

What is a hybrid car? It is any car that is powered by more than one source of energy. Electric motors, solar power and other technologies all have a part to play in the development of hybrid cars. Most hybrid cars on the road today are powered by a combination of an electric motor and a petrol engine. They are currently the most realistic alternative to a conventional car, because they do not have all the drawbacks of an electric car.

Full hybrid cars

The most common hybrid car is often called a 'full hybrid' car. It is powered by an electric motor alongside a conventional petrol engine. The electric motor can power the car on its own at low speed, such as when driving in a city. The combustion engine is used at higher speeds.

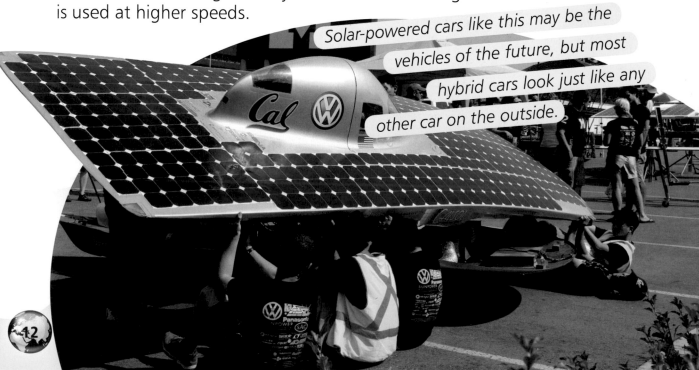

Solar-powered cars like this may be the vehicles of the future, but most hybrid cars look just like any other car on the outside.

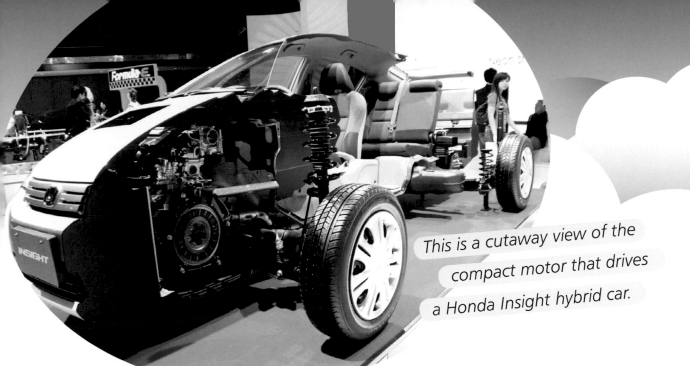

This is a cutaway view of the compact motor that drives a Honda Insight hybrid car.

Supermini hybrids

'Supermini hybrid' cars also have an electric motor, but it only provides extra power – the motor cannot power the car on its own. The electric motor helps to reduce the amount of fuel that the car uses.

Micro-hybrids

'Micro-hybrid' cars only make limited use of an electric motor. When the car is stopped at lights or in traffic, the combustion engine shuts off and an electric motor operates. When the car needs to move again, the motor means it is ready to start instantly. This saves a small amount of fuel.

ECO FACT

Travelling light

Although hybrid cars have both an internal combustion engine and an electric motor, they are much lighter than conventional cars. Hybrid cars have a much smaller engine. This reduces the weight of the car, and so less power is needed to push it along the road.

How hybrid cars work

All hybrid cars do not look the same under the bonnet. The motor industry is constantly developing new models of hybrid car that are more efficient. Most hybrid car drivetrains – the parts that combine to turn the wheels – fall into two different types: parallel and series.

The Toyota Prius was one of the first hybrid cars to become popular. This plug-in version can be recharged at home.

Parallel hybrids

Many of the most common hybrid cars, such as the Toyota Prius, operate with their two main power sources turning the same axle. Sometimes the petrol combustion engine will operate on its own. It may be supported by the electric motor when more power is needed, such as when the car is accelerating. Other parallel hybrids rely mostly on their electric motor, using the combustion engine only for driving on main roads. The car's combustion engine also charges the battery of the electric motor.

ECO FACT

Computer control

Computers have a big part to play in how hybrid and electric cars run. They decide when the car should use electric or petrol power and they monitor the car's performance.

This electric car made headlines when it won a race against 70 other cars.

The race was not to finish first but to see which car would use the least fuel to travel 92 kilometres.

Series hybrids

A series hybrid car includes an electric motor and a petrol-powered engine, but they are arranged differently from a parallel hybrid. Only the powerful electric motor is actually moving the car's wheels. The petrol engine is there just to recharge the electric motor. Series hybrid cars are also called Extended-Range Electric Vehicles (E-REV) because the engine helps them travel further but the main motor is fully electric.

Plug-in hybrids

One of the most recent developments in hybrid technology is the plug-in hybrid. This car is powered mainly by both a battery and an electric motor. Many car companies are developing plug-in hybrid cars, including BMW, Mitsubishi and Toyota.

The battery of the BMW i3 can be charged at home in less than 7 hours. An amazing 95 per cent of the car can be recycled.

Plug-in and go

Plug-in hybrids use their petrol engine only when their battery charge is below a certain level. This means that for most of the time they are electric cars, using no petrol and with no carbon dioxide emissions. They can be plugged into a home electricity supply, which will charge the battery pack.

Going the distance

Plug-in hybrids have one major benefit over a fully electric vehicle. A car that has only an electric motor cannot travel far between charges. This is not practical when people expect to be able to drive for several hours without stopping. Plug-in hybrids can be used on extended journeys because of their internal combustion engine, even if the engine is used less than in most hybrid cars.

Far from home, or the nearest charging point, power comes from a plug-in hybrid's internal combustion engine.

Making a choice

Many people expect plug-in hybrids to become more popular than other hybrid cars as technology improves, because they are the cheapest to run and have the lowest impact on the environment. But the plug-in cars available now are not very convenient. When plugged into an electricity supply, the batteries can take all night to charge fully. When drivers are deciding whether to buy a new car, they think about convenience as well as cost and the environment.

Using less fuel

Hybrid cars are usually more expensive than conventional cars of a similar size, but they are becoming more and more popular. In Japan, almost 20 per cent of new cars are hybrid vehicles. So what is the attraction?

A streamlined car with a low, rounded shape needs less fuel to move it through the air.

Saving money

As petrol prices rise, hybrid cars are becoming popular with drivers who want to reduce their fuel bills. A hybrid car's electric motor dramatically cuts the amount of petrol it uses. This will save money in the long-term, even though it costs a lot to buy a hybrid car.

Super efficient

Although electric cars are expensive to buy, their running costs are far lower than those of a conventional car. The most efficient electric cars on the road can cover almost 160 kilometres with an electric charge cost of around £2. To drive that distance in a conventional car would cost between £12 and £18.

Saving the environment

Hybrid cars are also bought by drivers who want to reduce the damage that cars do to the environment. Fumes from burning oil products, such as petrol or diesel, pollute the air. The build-up of these waste gases is causing Earth's climate to change. Hybrid vehicles cause less pollution than other vehicles.

Plug-in hybrids such as the Mitsubishi Outlander save money on petrol, but their owners will face higher electricity bills when charging the car's battery.

Fuel up close

There are several features of hybrid cars that allow them to use less fuel:
- Smaller engines are lighter and need less fuel.
- An electric motor takes over when the car is stopped or travelling at a lower speed, such as in a city.
- When a car brakes, energy is lost, but hybrid cars can recapture this to charge a battery.
- Streamlined designs reduce air resistance.

Reducing carbon emissions

In the United Kingdom, carbon dioxide from road transport makes up around 20 per cent of all greenhouse gas emissions. It makes up around 14 per cent in Australia. If a hybrid car uses half as much petrol as a conventional one, it will also produce half as much air pollution.

Biofuels are made from plants. They can be used in car engines, but there is not enough farmland on Earth to grow the biofuels we would need to replace oil.

Making a difference

Hybrid cars are a positive step, but we still have a long way to go in the fight against climate change. In 2013, nearly 33,000 hybrid and plug-in cars were sold in the United Kingdom. That sounds like a lot, but it is only a tiny fraction of the more than 2 million new cars bought that year. To date, Toyota have sold 50,000 of their hybrid cars in Australia, and predict greater sales in the future.

There are more than 1.35 billion people in China. At present, there is only one car for every 10 people in China, but cars are becoming much more popular.

More change needed

In many parts of the world, such as China and India, car ownership is growing fast and most of the cars sold have conventional engines. Unless hybrid cars become more affordable and more readily produced, climate change as a result of car pollution will continue to be a problem.

ECO FACT

Carbon caution

Hybrid and electric cars use less petrol than conventional cars, but they are only truly environmentally friendly if, rather than being run on electricity generated by the burning of fossil fuels, they are run on electricity generated from low-carbon sources. These include wind, solar and water power.

Hybrid car drawbacks

Hybrid cars can match conventional cars for speed and reliability. Cars driven by electric motors are much quieter. Most of all, hybrid and electric cars can save their owners money and help to reduce greenhouse gas emissions. So why doesn't everyone have a hybrid car?

Scientists are warning that the problems of climate change, such as melting ice sheets in the Arctic, far outweigh the drawbacks of switching to hybrid and electric cars.

ECO FACT

Too quiet?

Hybrid cars could have unexpected drawbacks. One complaint is that hybrid cars are too quiet. Cyclists or people crossing the street may not hear the cars coming. Some car companies have added extra noise to their cars to solve this problem.

Hybrid cars are becoming more commonplace in our cities. This hybrid car is being recharged on a city street.

Still costly

Hybrid cars are more expensive to buy than traditional cars. The reduced fuel costs act as an incentive to buy a hybrid, but there are other costs involved. All cars need regular servicing and maintenance. The systems that control hybrid cars are often very complex and people worry that the maintenance costs will be high.

Battery problems

The powerful batteries that drive hybrid and electric cars are being improved all the time but they still have some limits. A typical battery in a hybrid car needs charging every few days. Batteries do not always work as well in cold weather, so hybrid car users in cold countries find that they are using the petrol engine of their car more often.

High-speed hybrids

Hybrid cars are known for being clean but not much fun. That is all changing, as some of the world's most glamorous car companies are now releasing hybrid cars. High-speed hybrids use the latest hybrid technology to give them extra power and reduce fuel consumption.

The Porsche hybrid

Porsche is famous for making some of the world's fastest and most exciting cars. Now it is building hybrid cars. The company's 918 Spyder has a top speed of more than 320 kph and can accelerate from 0 to 100 kph in less than 3 seconds.

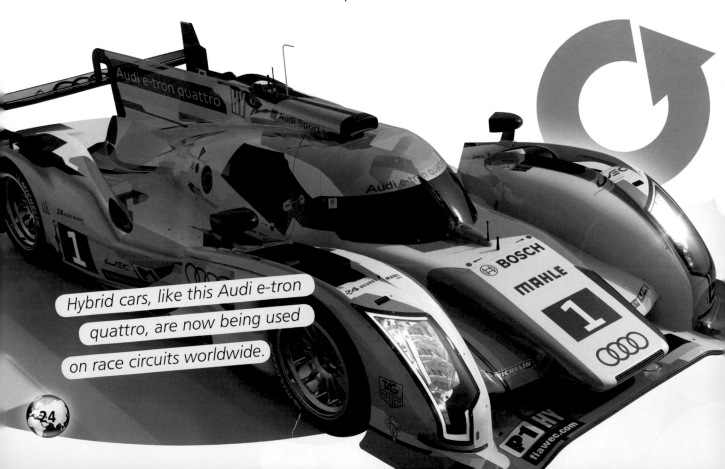

Hybrid cars, like this Audi e-tron quattro, are now being used on race circuits worldwide.

The Porsche 918 Spyder includes two electric motors alongside its powerful combustion engine, and Porsche claims the car can cover around 100 kilometres for every 3 litres of petrol it uses. The engine is used less, and so it uses less petrol. A conventional car uses around 8 litres of petrol for every 100 kilometres it travels.

From track to street

Costing more than £650,000, a car like the Porsche 918 Spyder is far too expensive for most drivers. However, technology and design features that are developed for use in supercars often influence the cars that the rest of us drive. These technologies will help to make hybrid cars faster, more efficient and more attractive to the average car owner.

More and more car owners will be driving hybrid cars in the future.

ECO FACT

Formula 1 future

Formula 1 racing cars now use Energy Recovery Systems (ERS) to regain the energy lost when they brake and then put it back into acceleration. There are also plans for cars to run just on battery power during pit stops.

The next step

Scientists are working on many alternative power sources for cars. None of these work as effectively as hybrid cars yet, but a breakthrough could change that.

For the moment, hybrid cars are the best solution for cleaner cars, but hydrogen or another power source may provide the key to road travel in the near future.

Power from the sun

The most powerful energy source available to us is the sun, and many experimental solar cars have been created. There are even races like the World Solar Challenge, in which solar cars race across Australia. However, storing energy for driving at night is a problem that has still not been solved. Solar cars are also currently very expensive to make.

Solar cells

Solar cars are powered by photovoltaic (PV) cells in solar panels. These cells convert energy from the sun into electricity. The cells absorb sunlight and use it to create a flow of particles called electrons. This flow can then be used to charge a battery.

Hydrogen power

Hydrogen-powered cars may be the solution. They use hydrogen and oxygen in cells to make electricity. The cells continue to produce power as long as they are kept supplied with hydrogen. One day we may all fill up at a hydrogen station.

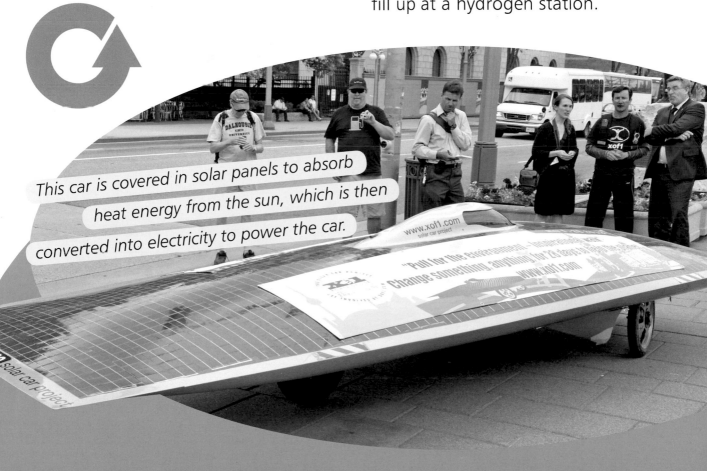

This car is covered in solar panels to absorb heat energy from the sun, which is then converted into electricity to power the car.

Fuel cells up close

Hydrogen fuel cells could power the cars of the future. The fuel cells combine hydrogen and oxygen, which is present in air, to make water. This process generates electricity to power the car. Hydrogen power is still in its early stages of development and the technology is not yet advanced enough for hydrogen powered cars to be widely available for public use.

Driving into the future

The future for cars is uncertain. Car ownership is increasing all the time, particularly in countries such as China and India. The number of cars on Earth could grow by 60 per cent over the next 20 years. At the same time, scientists are calling for urgent action to tackle climate change.

New fuels cannot offer a solution to road congestion. Public transport and other alternatives to cars may be the answer.

Hybrid heaven?

Some predict that, by 2030, around two-thirds of all new cars will be hybrid, plug-in hybrid or fully electric. Others think the numbers will be as low as 5 per cent. Rising petrol prices and government attempts to reduce carbon emissions will encourage people to make the switch.

New materials and design could mean the cars of the future look very different.

Super-light but tough materials will be developed using new technology so that cars will need less powerful engines. We will also see more cars that are driverless because they are operated by computers rather than by a driver. The computers will be programmed to drive the cars efficiently, thereby reducing their energy consumption.

Experimental engines

Experts hope that hydrogen-powered vehicles could lead a transport revolution, along with other fuels like ultra-cold liquid nitrogen, the gas that makes up most of Earth's atmosphere.

One thing we can be certain of is that the cars we will drive in the future will be very different.

Glossary

air resistance the ability to withstand the force of air

atmosphere the layer of gases surrounding Earth and containing the oxygen that humans and other animals breathe

axle a rod that is attached to the wheels of a car

carbon dioxide (CO_2) a greenhouse gas that is released when fossil fuels and organic matter are burned

carbon footprint the amount of greenhouse gas emissions caused by a single person or organisation

conventional normal or usual, such as conventional cars powered by an internal combustion engine

cylinder a hollow container, holding a piston, which forms part of an engine

diesel like petrol, a flammable product made from crude oil, which is used in internal combustion engines

drivetrains all the parts that work together to turn the wheels of cars

electrons small charged particles that are part of tiny atoms from which all matter is made

emissions the gases created by a car's engine and expelled through the exhaust

fossil fuels energy sources formed from the decayed remains of living things, including coal, oil and natural gas

generate to convert one form of energy into another, for example to produce electricity

greenhouse gas a gas that absorbs heat in the atmosphere

hydrogen a flammable gas that combines with oxygen to make water

internal combustion engine a type of engine in which motion is created by the burning of fossil fuels with air, as in a car

oxygen a gas that is part of Earth's atmosphere and which humans and other living things breathe

parallel hybrid a hybrid vehicle in which the wheels can be turned by either an internal combustion engine or electric motor

particles tiny objects, such as parts of atoms

petrol like diesel, a flammable product made from crude oil, which is used in internal combustion engines

photovoltaic (PV) cells cells that turn sunlight into electricity

series hybrid a hybrid car in which the wheels are driven by an electric motor alone, supported by a petrol engine

solar from the sun

For more information

Books

From the Model T to Hybrid Cars: How Transportation Has Changed, Jennifer Boothroyd, Lerner Publications

How Hybrid Cars Work, Jennifer Swanson, Child's World

Hybrid and Electric Vehicles, L.E. Carmichael, Essential Library

Victor Wouk: The Father of the Hybrid Car, Sean Callery, Crabtree

Websites

Discover more about how electric cars work at:
www.howstuffworks.com/electric-car.htm

This website tells you more about the solar-powered car race across Australia:
www.worldsolarchallenge.org

Learn about all kinds of 'green car', including hybrid, electric and hydrogen-powered, at:
www.which.co.uk/cars/choosing-a-car/car-features/ green-car-technologies-explained/green-cars-explained/

Index